Catholic Family Boot Camp

A 30 Day Devotional Workout

to Help Families Increase in Virtue

Mary Lou Rosien

Visit the author's website at

www.CatholicFamilyBootcamp.com

to join in on the great conversations, get discussion starter prompts for your family and enjoy boot camp updates and challenges for special times of the year such as Lent and Advent!

Published by

Bezalel Books

Waterford, MI

www.BezalelBooks.com

Printed in the United States of America

ISBN 978-1-936453-05-4

Library of Congress Catalog Control Number 2011905958

To My Family

you are my greatest blessing

I would like to thank my editor at Bezalel Books, Cheryl Dickow, for her encouragement and assistance in writing the book I always wanted to write. I would also like to thank my friend, and fellow author, Peggy Bowes, for her help in connecting me to Cheryl. Thanks to Lisa Mladinich and Cathy Dee, the editors for my monthly columns, for their support as well.

Many thanks to my darling husband, Igor, and sweet children: Daniel, Cameron, Katya, Nick, Andrew, Darya, Anya, and Vlad. I love you all more than words can say.

Thank you to my mom—who loves me to distraction and still teaches me daily; my sister, Amanda, brother, Joe, and their families.

And finally, a special thanks to my priests Fr. Joe and Fr. Lance, my mentor Dominic and all my special sisters in Christ. Note to Anne for always being my accountability partner, "I love you more than two dollars worth."

Dear Readers:

I have only one goal in providing you with this devotional book: to help your families increase in virtue.

We have a foster son in the military. When we sent him away to boot camp he came back physically and mentally stronger. He is now in Afghanistan fighting a fierce enemy. His training has proved valuable and strengthened him against the forces he must fight.

Families are fighting an enemy too. It is a strong, fierce enemy that attacks us through the media, in our schools, on the playgrounds and even sometimes in areas of worship. It seeks to destroy families! We must be strong in our Catholic Faith and in our families to be able to fight back.

Some have said that this book of active devotionals for families will be too difficult; that you will not invest the time and energy it takes to complete this challenge. They say that your lives are too busy to make this a priority. I disagree.

You are the families who get up before dawn to take your sons to football practice. The same families who cheer on your daughters while they play soccer in the pouring rain. You are the families who make the tough choice to home school, or work two jobs to send your kids to private school, or volunteer in your children's public schools to make them better. I know that your families are your priority and that you will do anything to strengthen them in this fight for faith over evil. I believe in you and you believe in each other.

I hope that this book helps you to achieve what your families are seeking. Good luck, God bless and many blessings!

In Christ,

Mary Lou Rosien

Lord, make me a channel of your peace;
where there is hatred, let me sow love;
where there is injury, your pardon Lord;
and where there's doubt, true faith in you;
O Master,
grant that I may not so much seek to be consoled as to console;
to be understood, as to understand;
to be loved, as to love;
for it is in giving that we receive,
it is in pardoning that we are pardoned,
and it is in dying that we are born to Eternal Life.

Prayer of St. Francis

Foreword

As a former Air Force pilot, I've been to boot camp, specifically at the Air Force Academy in Colorado Springs. That was the toughest six weeks of my life! I cried and I wanted to quit every day, but I knew that my hard work and determination would eventually pay off. Conquering boot camp was one of my greatest achievements.

My Catholic faith was also instrumental to my success during that difficult time. I prayed the Rosary on long marches in combat boots and went to Mass at the beautiful Academy chapel. These familiar rituals helped connect me to my family and served as a source of comfort.

I love that my friend Mary Lou has titled this book *Catholic Family Boot Camp*. Her program requires the same type of dedication and commitment as a military boot camp but is grounded in solid Catholic principles and virtues. She sets the bar high but gives families plenty of motivation and encouragement to persevere.

I had to be tough to make it through boot camp, but Mary Lou is much tougher than I am because she is the mother of seven children (and one foster son!). I think that anyone who can simply feed that many people breakfast every morning is highly qualified to run a boot camp. Mary Lou is organized, resourceful and creative. More importantly, she is grounded in her Catholic faith. She perfectly plays the role of the sensitive drill sergeant by setting high standards, providing the right tools for the job, and instilling confidence that success can be achieved. Mary Lou doesn't yell, humiliate or get in your face but generously shares her wisdom and experience in cultivating a holy family.

To make it through boot camp in the military, you must work as a team and you must train hard. The US military is the best in the world because it is built on teamwork that instills trust and on training that is repeated over and over until it's instinctive. Mary Lou clearly understands this concept because she devotes the very first day of her family boot camp to establishing a family team and choosing a name and slogan. She also encourages families to train hard, not in military maneuvers, but in cultivating virtue which must be practiced over and over until it becomes instinctive.

I look forward to implementing Mary Lou's terrific program with my own family because I know firsthand the benefits of a boot camp type of approach. There will probably be crying and someone will want to quit, but I will remind everyone about the rewards of hard work. I could not have become an Air Force pilot without first experiencing the rigors of boot camp. I know that conquering *Catholic Family Boot Camp* will be one of my family's greatest achievements.

Peggy Bowes
The Rosary Workout

Introduction

The Prayer of St. Francis has always been among my favorites. The focus is on the Theological and Cardinal Virtues as stated by the Catholic Church. These include the virtues of Faith, Hope, Charity/Love, Prudence, Justice, Fortitude and Temperance. This devotional will identify ways to increase these virtues in practical steps for family life.

To use this active devotional, I suggest first calling a family meeting and including all the members in what you are about to undertake. See if anyone has any concerns or questions and try to address them. Be flexible and open to possible concerns as well as determined in the face of reticence on any family member's part. Establish how the 30-day devotional will be carried out in the family. For example, you may have a few minutes each morning to share the task and the day's focus and then a few minutes again at night to share how the day went and wrap up with the prayer; or, you may do the "prep" work at night so that the next day will be spent on the task and the evening will thus be both a review of the day's focus plus the prep for the following day. Again, this is about making a concerted effort to give your family both the time and the tools to increase in virtue!

Use something like a small dry-erase board and each day write down the task and the Scripture verse that accompanies it. Make sure the board is in a location where all family members can see it and thus be reminded of the task at hand. In this devotional, the task is written in italic for each day's entry and the Scripture verse is written underneath the task.

It looks like this:

Hope ~ Boot Camp Day 2: Getting onto the Same Page
Task: Plan a family retreat day.

"By wisdom a house is built, and by understanding it is established; And by knowledge the rooms are filled with precious and pleasant riches." Proverbs 24:3-4

You will see that each day the virtue is identified—in the example above, the virtue is "hope" and the day of the devotional is "2." The focus in this example is "Getting on the Same Page" and taken in context it is referring to gathering family members together and working as a team. The task is "Plan a family retreat day." You can see that the Scripture verse applicable is from Proverbs.

Give every person a small notebook to journal their thoughts and responses to the tasks. Have older siblings help young siblings with their writing and sharing. And by all means, make up tasks as the Spirit moves you! This devotional is meant to be a tool for families to shape their lives in a virtuous way and you will undoubtedly read a day's entry and see ways that you can ask your family to apply it in your own home, in your unique circumstances. The tasks shared are either your starting point or simply your example.

If you have opted to begin the day with the identification of the task, you'll also want to read the short entry to the family. If you are doing this in the evening, you will be reading the entry for what will be the next day's focus and task while also discussing the tasks of that particular day. Again, this is about what will work for your family so there is a lot of flexibility.

In addition to tasks, throughout the devotional you will find other activities and information. You will see there is a worksheet that goes with the finance task and other worksheets as well. There are specific examples of how to pray with the family while there are also some techniques for improving communication within your family.

Each new virtue that is tackled begins with a short definition and then the devotion continues with an emphasis on that particular trait development

Everything in this devotional—in this "boot camp"—is meant to be a seed that is planted and will continue to grow long after the 30-day devotional itself has been completed!

A final, personal note: I've started a website which has forums for you to share your own experiences—successes and even failures—and interact with other families that are attending "boot camp." I hope you will come and find wisdom, offer support and make this a life-changing event for yourself and for others! We're here:

http://www.catholicfamilybootcamp.com

God bless,
Mary Lou Rosien

The overall devotional at a glance:

Virtue	Day	Task
Hope	1	Name your team and decide on a family mantra
Hope	2	Plan a family retreat day
Hope	3	Look at your family with a realistic view
Hope	4	Devote family prayers for the needs of one family member
Hope	5	By this point someone may be getting tired of doing the 30 days and has started working against it; tackle the problem head-on
Love	6	Invest in each family member and what is important to them: hopes, dreams and even fears
Love	7	Try to find, understand and meet a need in your family members
Love	8	Make a list of each family member and next to their name write down one of their greatest gifts
Love	9	Protect a family member's weakness
Love	10	Make a list of things for which you are grateful
Love	11	Allow your love for Christ and His love for you transform you
Justice	12	Forgive a family member for something and ask for forgiveness in return
Justice	13	Make restitution for a wrong you have done
Justice	14	Go to Confession as a family
Justice	15	Have a family meeting about attitudes regarding finances and giving to charity
Justice	16	Have a second family meeting to discuss specifics of handling money and financial goals
Prudence	17	Return with love a habit that is driving you crazy
Prudence	18	Change your attitude about something you don't like
Prudence	19	Start targeting specific individual behaviors that are getting the way of family unity; make a plan to change these behaviors
Temperance	20	Choose to be kind when someone is not treating you kindly
Temperance	21	Practice a behavior you are trying to change
Temperance	22	Discuss developing an attitude of chastity with your family
Fortitude	23	Do a favor for someone in your family and tell them it is to express appreciation
Fortitude	24	Review methods of discipline in your family and their effectiveness or ineffectiveness
Fortitude	25	Make a choice not to yell today
Fortitude	26	Introduce a new way of communicating to your family
Faith	27	Make prayer a priority
Faith	28	Go to Mass as a family
Faith	29	Study Scripture as a family
Faith	30	Have a recommitment ceremony consecrating your family to the Sacred Heart of Jesus through the Immaculate Heart of Mary

Focus is on the Virtue of Hope (Days 1 through 5)

Perhaps you are starting this journey because your family seems out of step with each other. Maybe you are interested in strengthening your family's core or just drawing closer to one another. Hope in the Lord can help you to hope in each other.

Hope ~ Boot Camp Day 1: Go Team!
Task: Name your team and decide on a family mantra.

"For this reason...the two shall be as one." Eph. 5:31

The Name Game

Think about what might happen if a Washington Redskin football player was traded to the Buffalo Bills. Would that player be a team player if he still wore his Redskins jersey? Didn't Batman and Superman become even stronger as members of the "Justice League?" A team name takes on new importance when viewed like this.

I, myself, grew up with a hyphenated name. Oddly enough, in my case it has been my family name since the 1800's. Although I did love my family name, it was often a source of confusion. I was misaddressed, people dropped either the first or last part of my unusual name, and it was difficult. My name had 13 letters and a hyphen; it never fit on any form. Years later, my father left and my mother remarried, then my name was different from my mother's. Talk about confusion! When my maternal grandparents stayed with us, we had three last names in the same household. While I did not suffer any damage from all the confusion, I am not sure it would be a good thing to *intentionally* put a child through.

By contrast, when my husband, Igor, grew up his entire family had the same last name. It was a source of pride to all of them. They were told, "A Rosien would never···" or, "A Rosien always···" There was a strong sense of belonging to something bigger than themselves. Something permanent, that went back through the ages. It is because of this that we have dubbed our family the "Rosien team" or "Team Rosien."

However, if your family is blended, or for whatever reason there are many last names in the household (we have a foster son, so we have that situation too), perhaps consider a family nickname. Give your family team a name you can all share—or make a commitment to the name you do share.

Family Slogan

Having a family code of honor or slogan is a great tool to increase family solidarity and strength. This helps teach your children the values of your family. Reflect on how the branches of the military use this technique to create a sense of unity and give the team a common goal. While we can't always control the last names we have in any given family, we can agree to a code of honor or a mantra that states who we are and what we believe. Talk about what the family name means to each of you and ways that you each will "own" it and take responsibility for honoring it.

PRAYER

Lord, by our Baptisms we are all part of Your family. Help us to remember that our last name is *Christian* and following your commandments is our code of honor.

Hope ~ Boot Camp Day 2: Getting onto the Same Page

Task: Plan a family retreat day.

"By wisdom a house is built, and by understanding it is established; And by knowledge the rooms are filled with precious and pleasant riches." Proverbs 24:3-4

At one particular time in our marriage, we felt that our family life was not on track. Our solution was to create a *family team building retreat*. We took the children out of school (which united them in playing hooky), we set up a system in which we had two teams (boys v. girls), we (the parents) were the score keepers, we then did a variety of team centered activities (went bowling, out for ice cream, etc.) while secretly keeping score of the positive and negatives that each team did. The idea was to help the children see themselves as team members and encourage them to work together. Oddly enough, the two teams tied at the end of the day and everyone was rewarded.

Even the most difficult or most enjoyable areas of our lives can be used for team building. A big part of family cohesiveness is the ability to play together. The overall goal is not complicated: create a happy, healthy environment for families to grow. Hidden opportunities are everywhere; it is all in your point of view.

PRAYER

Lord, you designed our family, you knew the children we needed and the parents they needed. Remind us to enjoy our "team time."

Family Goal Worksheet

What order would we put these issues?

Work _____

Prayer _____

God _____

Volunteering or Service _____

Time with Friends _____

Time Alone _____

Taking Vacations _____

Money _____

The goals for our family are:

_____ in 6 months.

_____ in 1 year.

_____ in 5 years.

_____ in 10 years.

_____ in 20 years.

Hope ~ Boot Camp Day 3: Great Expectations
Task: Look at your family with a realistic view.

"May the Lord direct your hearts to the love of God and to the endurance of Christ." 2 Thes. 3:5

I was frustrated with the messy house. My husband was frustrated with the noise, and the kids were frustrated with each other. All of this revolved around unrealistic expectations.

We have six kids still at home; my house (no matter how I try) will never look like a magazine picture. We will have noise around us for years and the kids will argue. Realizing the reality in which we live can help us have more realistic expectations about our life together.

I have a friend who is a professor of economics. He works with numbers all day long. So when his seven children were driving him a little bonkers at church (due to their interruptions) he decided to work it out statistically. He took the number of children, their ages and the length of Mass and figured out what a realistic number of interruptions would be. Much to his surprise, his kids were actually causing fewer interruptions than the statistical probability! This knowledge helped him adjust his expectations during Mass and he felt calmer and less irritated by his children's behavior.

In our family, we often react with frustration when our daughter (with disabilities) doesn't "act her age;" and yet the reality is that she may be incapable of "acting her age." When we remember this, we are less likely to respond to her in an inappropriate or disproportionate way.

We all harbor unrealistic expectations either from pride, ignorance or because we just haven't looked at the situation correctly. Keeping this in check will help us live more harmoniously.

<u>PRAYER</u>
Lord, open our eyes and help us to be realistic about our family expectations. Help us to focus more on acceptance than perfection.

Hope ~ Boot Camp Day 4: We Are Not Alone in Suffering

Task: Devote family prayers for the needs of one family member.

"All things are possible with God." Mark 10:27

All families struggle with issues. In our family, two of our sons have struggled with their faith. We have also been through the pain of a child leaving home on bad terms. Families deal with alcoholism, drug addiction, violence, unplanned pregnancy and other difficult situations. It is easy to feel helpless in any one of those situations and even to doubt the decisions we made as parents.

We can pray, though. Not just throwing up a quick prayer, but turning our active attention to prayer. Pray scripture out loud, especially the Psalms or the Book of Job, which are both filled with the heartfelt sufferings of the authors. My mother is a wonderful example to us. She offers up sacrifices for us and regularly participates in Novenas for me, my siblings and our families.

We can tie our sufferings to Christ on the cross and to the Blessed Mother at the foot of that cross. It is so easy to feel like we are alone when we suffer. To remind us that we are not, we can meditate on the cross and unite our difficulties to Christ and His Blessed Mother. They feel our pain and they pray with us and for us.

PRAYER
Lord, we do suffer severely at times. Help us to remember that we do not suffer alone and that prayer can change even the most difficult situations. Nothing is impossible with You.

Hope ~ Boot Camp Day 5: Problem Solving

Task: By this point someone may be getting tired of doing the thirty days and has started working against it; tackle the problem head-on.

"But make sure this liberty of yours in no way becomes a stumbling block to the weak." 1 Cor. 8:9

Psychologist, Aimee O'Connell states, "When I'm coaching a team that's gotten unruly and disrespectful of one another, I'll have a team meeting."

She suggests a specific strategy to overcome problems:

- ✓ Identify those players who are the chief antagonists and then meet with each of them individually.
- ✓ Listen to what they have been experiencing and what's behind all their difficult behavior.
- ✓ Validate anything that is legitimately upsetting them.
- ✓ Ask them what their needs are and develop a plan to meet those needs.
- ✓ Remind them that they need to find appropriate ways to get their needs met and that the disruptive behavior must stop.
- ✓ Meet with other members of the team to give them validation and support.

Using this method to solve issues early can lead to a team that functions positively and makes progress in all areas of family life.

PRAYER
Lord, help us to know when we have become each other's stumbling block. Help us to address and correct this behavior in our family.

Before moving on to Love, insights from the family boot camp activities on Hope:

_____
_____
_____
_____
_____
_____
_____
_____
_____
_____
_____
_____
_____
_____

Focus is on the Virtue of Charity or Love (Days 6 through 11)

The Catholic Church teaches that Charity and Love are one in the same. When we love, we are charitable—and vice versa. Sometimes it can seem much more difficult to be charitable to those in our own families than it is to be loving to strangers. This section will help to refocus efforts to be a loving person, family member and citizen.

Love ~ Boot Camp Day 6: Becoming an Expert on Family Members
Task: Invest in each family member and what is important to them: hopes, dreams, even fears.

"How blessed is the man who finds wisdom, and the man who gains understanding." Proverbs 3:13

As my friend Tina Feigal, M.S., Ed., Parent Coach/Trainer says, "Your home is your science laboratory." My husband, the scientist (physician and amateur astronomer), reminds me that *observation* is the biggest part of learning. Each family member learns differently, reacts to correction in his/her own way and has unique interests. For instance, two of my daughters play soccer. They both love the game, but play it in their own style. Katya enjoys offense, but thrives on defense. Her face becomes determined and flushed as soon as she sees the ball coming toward her team's goal. Darya, on the other hand, loves offense. She wants to assist on every goal. She is a strong team player and can't wait till she makes a goal. Same game, different views.

One of my core beliefs about love, family and relationships is that, *when you love someone, you become an expert on them.* I have been married for a long time, and yet I still learn new things about my husband every day. Spending time actively observing family members, and asking questions about their lives helps us to love each other more. What are our hopes, dreams, and fears? What really makes each of us happy or sad?

It is not enough to just be present; we have to watch our children. My son, Andrew, has a temper like mine. He gets very angry for a short time. Blows off steam. Apologizes and gets over it. Nick and Katya are more like their dad. They can stew about something for hours. They need processing time and can't be rushed to say they are sorry, forgive the other person and move on. Neither approach is wrong, just different.

This year as a family, we decided to recognize and support one of each of our dreams. My son, Nick, loves to do BMX biking. So this year we gave up some things to save money for him to attend a BMX camp for a week. Our fourteen year-old daughter, Darya, wanted to learn to ice skate, so dad gives up an hour and a half on the weekend to take her skating. We are supporting our daughter, Katya's, dream to pursue a career as a photographer by sending her to college and supplementing that by some workshops in photography. Anya wanted to try out for the school play, so Mom played taxi driver for months driving her back and forth to school, because Anya is afraid to ride the late bus. It is amazing how the children responded to us supporting their dreams, especially when they recognized that time or finances made it difficult to do so.

People do not remain the same. As their lives change, so do they. Watching, asking and learning about family members helps us love each other more.

<u>PRAYER</u>

Lord, what are we *not* noticing in our own family? Does someone have a need we are not meeting or a fear that we are ignoring? Help us to know each other better so that we can love each other more fully.

Love ~ Boot Camp Day 7: Not to be Understood and to Understand
Task: Try to find, understand and meet a need in your family members.

"He laid down His life for us. We should also lay down our lives for our brothers." 1 John 3:16

Perhaps our youngest daughter has been shouting more lately because she has a need we are not meeting? Is our middle son difficult right now because of changes in his adolescent body, or are we missing an unmet need? How do we figure it all out?

We decided that we needed to observe family members more closely, talk with them, and understand what their current struggles are. Singer/Songwriter, Marie Bellet, has a line in a song about her husband that goes, "He'd like to find the news and just get lost, but in one heroic moment, he says come sit with me. He gathers them to him as he turns off the TV." I think this demonstrates the ability to guage your families' needs and put your own needs aside for them.

There is an old saying that *when someone acts unlovable, that is when they need love the most.* Uncovering the reasons for someone's stressful behavior and filling those needs will be a constant challenge for our family, but one worth undertaking.

PRAYER

Lord, so many times we feel like we have needs that are not being met. Help all of us to live the Prayer of St. Francis and focus more on loving others and filling their needs than on our own needs.

Love ~ Boot Camp Day 8: There Is No Appendix in the Body of Christ

Task: Make a list of each family member and beside their name write down one of their greatest gifts.

"You formed my inmost being; you knit me in my mother's womb. I praise you, so wonderfully you made me; wonderful are your works."
Psalm 139: 13,14

I was holding my ten year-old daughter close to me one Sunday, as I listened to the reading,

"For just as the body is one and has many members, and all the members of the body, though many, are one body, so it is with Christ. For in one Spirit we were all baptized into one body···

···If the foot should say, "Because I am not a hand, I do not belong to the body," that would not make it any less a part of the body. And if the ear should say, "Because I am not an eye, I do not belong to the body," that would not make it any less a part of the body···

But as it is, God arranged the members in the body, each one of them, as he chose. If all were a single member, where would the body be? As it is, there are many parts, yet one body.

The eye cannot say to the hand, "I have no need of you," nor again the head to the feet, "I have no need of you···Now you are the body of Christ and individually members of it." 1 Corinthians 12:12-27

This suddenly became significant to me in a way that it had not before. My daughter is moderately cognitively delayed and has a mild form of Autism. She is prone to outbursts and her behavior often mimics a child of a much younger age. I love her intensely, but I won't pretend that at times I am not frustrated or even angered by her behavior. Going to church can be especially difficult for us. She talks, wiggles and demands my attention. I struggle with paying attention to the Mass while trying not to respond negatively to her behavior. Added to that, is the fact that people around us can't see her disabilities, only her bad behavior. I admit at times it is very embarrassing. Holding her during that reading, I realized that God did not create any useless members in the Body of Christ. My sweet little girl has a purpose. I began to meditate on the purpose of each individual.

I know that in my family, my daughter has taught us all patience. It is not unusual during one of her meltdowns for her to get 'locked in' with one of us. At that point there are no visible solutions. She screams and cries. She demands help and says that you are wrong when you give help. Yet, often one of her siblings will step in to try and diffuse her meltdown. At times the worst in her brings out the best in them.

My little girl also plays the clarinet quite well. Is that her gift in the Body of Christ? She has a huge capacity to love, perhaps that is the gift the Lord will use. I cannot know what the future will hold, but I know that she has a job, a place and a purpose in God's plan and in His body. We all do.

PRAYER
Lord, we sometimes forget the worth of those in our own family. Help us to remember that You created each of us for a special purpose.

Love ~ Boot Camp Day 9: Don't Ask, Don't Tell
Task: Protect a family member's weaknesses.

> *"She opens her mouth in wisdom, and on her tongue is kindly counsel." Proverbs 31:26*

I have long believed that protecting each other is an important piece of marriage and family relationships. When we reveal one another's vulnerabilities with others, we are exposing them to the world. I am amazed, and saddened, at how often I have heard this done.

The wife who complains endlessly about her husband's faults to her girlfriends, or the husband who shares intimate details of his relationship with his wife, damages that relationship. This is also true in families. When talking to others we must always protect the sanctity of our marriage and our families. We must resist the temptation to participate in conversations that put down our family members, expose their vulnerabilities or conversations that attack family life in general. When you love someone you do everything you can to protect them; you do not leave them open to the criticism of the world.

My oldest daughter and next youngest son (who fought through their early teens) have learned the value of protecting each other's secrets. Recently, our daughter said that she had heard something worrisome about her brother, but she wouldn't say what it was. Her reason was that he would not trust her again if she shared it and she would rather find out the truth first, than to destroy his trust in her without reason. I was very proud of her. She is a smart and loving girl and I knew that she would talk to her brother, guide him with good advice and bring us into the issue if he was in real trouble. As it turns out, her concerns were not justified and they were able to discuss the whole issue. What a gift, to have children who can trust each other, go to each other for advice and pray for each other when needed.

PRAYER

Lord, help us to know what secrets to keep and when to call in help. Let that 'help' always start with a prayer to you for guidance.

Love ~ Boot Camp Day 10: Attitudes of Gratitude
Task: Make a list of things you are grateful for.

"I never stop thanking God for all the graces you have received."
1 Cor. 1:4

When we feel that we have lost sight of what we should be grateful for, we play 'Gratitudes and bad-a-tudes!' Our good friends, the Schwalms, gave us this great idea. Each person shares his/her high and low point of the day. Often the children will mention their own bad behavior as their bad-a-tude. This is a great opportunity for self reflection, reconciliation and self-monitoring. We are often surprised that their gratitude is for something another family member did for them.

Counting our blessings reminds us that, in spite of difficult times, we have a lot to be grateful for. It is easy in stressful times to forget just how many things are going right for us. Maybe we are suffering from unemployment, but friends have graced us with dinner or support. We could be facing a serious health problem, but have a good doctor involved with our care. There is almost always some gift in a difficult situation if we look hard enough.

PRAYER

Lord, we often get caught up in how hard things are for us. Help us to see the blessings that you give us every day and to remember to thank you for them.

Love ~ Boot Camp Day 11: Brand New

Task: Allow your love for Christ and His love for you to transform you.

"I will put in them a new heart and put a new spirit within them."
Ezekiel 11:19

Ugh. I started out today so badly! My daughter screamed at me (my youngest girl with the Asperger's and delays); and, like an idiot, I finally screamed back.

Then, my older daughter, hearing my frustration, came down and was kind to her little sister. (At that point, the little one was completely locked in and melting down, hence my own meltdown.) My older daughter had just met someone special and I couldn't help but think how my older daughter's new-found love was giving her extraordinary patience. She had been transformed by love.

Isn't that what I am supposed to do? I am called to use the extraordinary graces the Lord provides to care for my children, even when—especially when—they try my patience. Shouldn't the love I have in my heart for the Lord transform me the same way my daughter's new love had transformed her?

PRAYER

Lord, You so often taught us with soft words of truth—or no words at all. Help us control our tongues and not to speak in anger, even when we feel provoked.

Before moving on to Justice, insights from the family boot camp activities on Love:

_____

_____

_____

_____

_____

_____

_____

Focus is on the Virtue of Justice (Days 12 through16)

It is said that the virtue of Justice perfects the will. It reminds us of the dignity of each human being and encourages us to pay our debts. All this is part of normal family life.

Justice ~ Boot Camp Day 12: It's Not Okay
Task: Forgive a family member for something and ask for forgiveness in return.

"Be kind to one another, compassionate, forgiving one another as God has forgiven you in Christ."
Eph. 4:32

Our family once had a forgiveness ceremony. Each person divided a paper in two and wrote something someone had done to hurt them on one side and something they had done to hurt another family member on the other side. We tore off the thing someone had done to hurt us and placed it into a bowl. Then we burned them and vowed to let go of past hurts.

We continued by reading the thing we were sorry for to the person we had hurt and asked for forgiveness. We have always had the rule in our home, that if someone says, "I'm sorry," the response cannot be, "It's okay," because it is not acceptable or "okay" to hurt. The response must be, "I forgive you."

This had a tremendous effect on all of us. We felt it was important to combine the two ideas because the Our Father states, "Forgive us our trespasses as we forgive those who trespass against us." We wanted to look at both sides of this.

This exercise had one amazing outcome. My son apologized for something that he had done months ago to hurt his dad. My husband then confessed that the very thing my son apologized for was the thing he had written down and burned. They both had tears in their eyes as they recognized the anger and pain they had just released.

Maybe the saying that "Forgiveness is a gift you give yourself" isn't entirely true. Offering and accepting forgiveness heals all involved. It is a gift you can give someone you love.

PRAYER
Lord, teach us to live the words in the Our Father and to forgive the same way we wish to be forgiven.

Justice ~ Boot Camp Day 13: Payback

Task: Make restitution for a wrong you have done.

"...go first and be reconciled with your brother..." Matthew 5:24

Q: Why do I have to tell a priest my sins? I can just tell God I am sorry. What does the Church teach about the Sacrament of Reconciliation?

A: First of all, it is a celebration. Who wouldn't want to attend a joyous celebration? Secondly, on your own, you cannot be sure of perfect contrition. If you are not perfectly sorry, how can you be sure that you are forgiven? (*CCC #1453*) In Reconciliation, our contrition is made perfect. We are *assured* forgiveness *and* we are reminded to thank God for it. This helps us grow in humility and decrease in pride. Third, we are not, "telling our sins to a priest." The priest is giving us the ear of Christ to whisper in. He is taking the visible place of Christ, but Christ is there.

"You owe me a good!" My husband, Igor, instituted this system of penance for all of us. When one person in our family hurts another in any way, the offending party owes the other a 'good.' This means he/she must render a favor to the hurt party upon request. This system has helped all of us monitor our behavior and make repentance for any injury.

Sometimes we think that saying we are sorry is enough to undo the pain we have caused by our behavior; it's not. We have to rebuild trust, to show that we are truly sorry for the mistake that we have made. Talk is cheap, actions are harder.

I am as guilty of this as anyone else. I'll mutter an apology without any real commitment to changing my behavior. Doing a 'good' makes me take responsibility for my actions.

PRAYER

Lord, open our eyes to the times we have hurt each other and help us to heal that hurt.

Justice ~ Boot Camp Day 14: Clean and Sparkly

Task: Go to Confession as a family.

"Therefore, confess your sins to one another and pray for one another, that you may be healed." James 5:16

When our kids were little we liked to pile them into our big, 15-passenger van, after a long, dirty winter—and go to the car wash. The children found it thrilling, a little scary and really cool! It reminds me, a little, of the need to go to confession regularly. None of us wants the dirt and salt to destroy our cars, and yet, do we think about our souls in the same way?

Reasons for Reconciliation···

- As the saying goes: "The family that prays together stays together."
- We are strengthened by Actual Grace (helps us to make good choices) and renewed by Sanctifying Grace (brings us closer to God).
- We develop good habits. Going to confession can be a little scary at first, but like anything else, if we do it often, it becomes comfortable. Receiving the Sacrament of Reconciliation should be something we anticipate with joy and a sense of celebration as part of our Catholic Faith.
- We develop and maintain an informed conscience.
- We are made strong by putting on our armor against a world full of temptation.
- The Sacrament of Reconciliation saves marriages and family relationships.
- When one person in a marriage sins, the effects are felt by both—because they truly are one. As we are reconciled to the Lord, we are reconciled to one another.

How often should we go···Every month is suggested whereas every week would be wonderful; but every year is required according to Church law, *CCC #1457.* By holding ourselves accountable, we may be better inclined to try to change wrong behavior.

Do we allow sin to build up and destroy the beauty of God's grace life within us? My family has found that making the Sacrament of Reconciliation a family affair can be like the car wash: thrilling, sometimes a little scary and really cool!

Jesus himself instituted the Sacrament of Confession and the priesthood. "Amen, I say to you, whatever you bind on earth will be bound in heaven, and whatever you loose on earth shall be loosed in heaven." Matt 18:18

Jesus also states, "Receive the holy Spirit. Whose sins you forgive are forgiven them and whose sins you retain are retained." John 20:22-23

In the *Catechism of the Catholic Church #1457* we are reminded that, "···after having attained the age of discretion, each of the faithful is bound by an obligation faithfully to confess serious sins at least once a year." We are instructed by the Church to go to confession whenever we have committed a mortal sin and furthermore, to confess venial sins.

So the next time we are at church and see all those shiny, clean cars in the parking lot, we may want to ask ourselves, "Is my soul as clean as my car?"

PRAYER

Lord, You are so forgiving and are waiting for us in the Sacrament of Reconciliation. Help us to utilize this sacrament and to teach our children to love it, too. Thank you for the gift of your forgiveness through this sacrament.

Justice ~ Boot Camp Day 15: Money Talk
Task: Have a family meeting about attitudes regarding finances and giving to charity.

"For those others have all made offerings from their surplus wealth, but she, from her poverty, has offered her whole livelihood."
Luke 21:4

A friend's 3 year-old daughter, Sarah, watched carefully as her daddy put money in the basket every week at Mass. Then, on her birthday, she received a crisp twenty dollar bill in the mail. "Look," she exclaimed, "Money for the church basket."

Finances are one of the issues that many families avoid talking about, and it causes some of the greatest conflict. There are ways to turn this negative into a positive. Having a family meeting to discuss attitudes about money, financial goals and struggles can help the family approach finances with a team attitude.

Families can begin discussing finances by looking at their habits, strengths and weaknesses around money issues. Consider each spouse's comfort level with money. For example, maybe the husband is a great money manager, but the whole process of paying the bills stresses him out terribly. It is vitally important for a couple to understand their *feelings* about money in order to make an appropriate plan for the family.

A helpful thing to consider when looking at financial issues is what the Church advises. We should always give our first fruits to the Lord. Many people have difficulty accepting this, especially when they first start out and have very little. However, if we consider that *everything* we have comes from God and He only requests a small portion of that back, it makes it easier to give. If a couple is really financially strapped, then they may want to look at contributing to their church in another way. Perhaps they can donate time. They could help run the church's youth group, teach religion, or drive an elderly person to Mass on Sundays and holy days of obligation.

When we give joyfully we can teach our children an attitude of giving and tithing by our own example.

PRAYER
Lord, help us to be like the poor widow, willing to give from our hearts without restriction.

Justice ~ Boot Camp Day 16: Show Me the Money

Task: Have a second family meeting to discuss the specifics of handling money and financial goals.

"Let your life be free from love of money but be content with what you have, for he has said, 'I will never forsake or abandon you.'"
Hebrews 13:5

We were going on a family vacation and our younger children wanted some spending money. I had a messy basement and wanted it cleaned. So, we had the children go through the toys they weren't using and have their own garage sale. We allowed them to set prices, run the sale (with supervision) and keep the money that they made.

Simple tips can help us to get finances under control:

- ✓ Evaluate spending. For example, as our children have gotten older, our grocery bill has grown. We never needed to really consider groceries a bill, but now we find it is our largest monthly expenditure. Gas prices have gone up and we added two new drivers this year, so we need to look at their insurance and gas costs, too.
- ✓ Establish a goal (i.e. saving for a house, getting out of debt, saving for additional schooling, etc). Discussing who is the most frugal or who handles money well is crucial. Children can be involved in the process of setting financial goals and learning to save for them.
- ✓ Avoid debt at all costs. It is not necessary to start out life with a new car, a home, and a lot of things. Credit card use should be limited if they are used at all. Some of our happiest times were when we were broke and struggling. It is in getting through those times that families learn to function as a team.
- ✓ Making good buying choices is another way to promote good financial habits and to team build. If you desire something, save for it and buy it when you can afford it. We recently bought a used car off a computer site rather than get into debt on a new car. We could afford new car payments, but a new car was not really necessary. I would rather own nothing new and have no debt, then to live like kings and not really own anything at all. This outlook keeps us safe. If we fell apart financially tomorrow we would lose very little.
- ✓ Consider selling what you don't need. The fastest way to get out of debt is to get rid of what you don't need. Selling the car you can't afford and getting a cheaper one may lead to much less stress in your marriage. Having a garage sale to bring in a little extra cash may take some pressure off the two of you as a couple. Building up

treasures in heaven and not on earth can be a freeing prospect.

✓ Find hidden money for things you need or to bring down debt. Maybe brown bagging lunch could save a family $ 5.00 a day, that adds up to $100.00 on an average work month.

✓ Establish a plan. In the example discussed earlier, perhaps the solution could be for the husband to make a monthly family budget and the wife to write out the bills each month. The husband's strength would be utilized while his anxiety is diminished. If a family is currently in debt they should decide which bills they will overpay slightly every month and get rid of that debt over time. Being honest about money issues can strengthen the team and lessen the opportunities for conflict.

PRAYER

Lord, help us to be good stewards of what you have entrusted to us. Guide us in our financial lives as well as all other areas of our lives.

Where do we want to be financially in?

6 months   _____

1 year   _____

5 years   _____

10 years   _____

Overall Financial Goal   _____

What would we give up to accomplish financial goals? (examples: no vacations for 5 years in order to buy a home, saving for furniture rather than going out for dinner for one year, working to save for two years so my spouse can stay home with the children once they are born, moving to a smaller house so my husband can work less hours, etc.)

_____

_____

_____

Financial Work Sheet

Assets

Savings account balance _____

Checking account balances _____

_____

Other assets _____

_____

Total assets _____

Debt; Bills

Mortgage/Rent _____

Gas/Electric _____

Phone _____

Cell phones _____

Computer hook up _____

Car loans _____

_____

Other loans _____

_____

TV Cable company _____

_____

Charitable giving _____

Gas _____

Food _____

Misc. _____

_____

Total Monthly Bills _____

Monthly Income less Monthly Bills

= Net Monthly Income: _____

Savings each month _____

Extra towards debt _____

Time to assess progress ...

Where are our successes? Where do we need to improve? What are we learning about ourselves and one another?

_____
_____
_____
_____
_____
_____
_____
_____
_____
_____
_____
_____
_____
_____
_____
_____
_____
_____
_____
_____
_____
_____
_____
_____
_____
_____
_____
_____

Focus is on the Virtue of Prudence (Days 17 through19)

The virtue of Prudence perfects the intellect and helps us use wisdom to discern situations. This virtue is valuable in avoiding sin and determining the gifts of individuals within a family.

Prudence ~ Boot Camp Day 17: Family First

Task: Seeing things in a new light and with love.

"Strive for peace with everyone, and for that holiness without which no one will see the Lord."
Hebrews 12:14

In marriage, little things can be blown out of proportion. It took me five years into our life together to realize that my husband may never remember to shut his closet door or close his dresser drawers. This habit used to drive me nuts. Then, one day, I discovered that I had been missing an opportunity to show love to him and increase the grace in our marriage. I began to mentally give him a kiss each time I closed a closet or shut a drawer. This tiny practice allowed me to stop nagging and actually smile when I saw the clothes hanging out of his dresser. How we react to any habit is really up to us, not our spouse or children. We can't change them, but we can change ourselves.

When I remember to be of service to my husband and anticipate his needs, our marriage flourishes. I change my thinking from, "How come he can't help me get the kids ready for Mass and watch them there?" to, "He (my husband) worked so hard last night; I want to let him sleep in. I am able to bathe the kids and save a little time in getting ready for Mass, which will help the morning progress smoothly. I have the rest of the week at home to pray, listen to the Catholic radio station or tapes, he will really benefit from being able to relax and listen to the Homily, I will care for the younger ones." Instead of a list of things *I did*, I am able to give my husband gifts, freely and with a full heart.

When we are 'other' focused we find that selfishness decreases and selflessness increases. My husband repays me for my acts of love by countless acts of his own. When we are both trying to please the other we are both happier and less focused on our own needs. This helps us both to move along the path to holiness. This example teaches our children to try to think of others (including their siblings) first.

PRAYER

Lord, do our bad habits drive You crazy? We make mistakes and yet you forgive us and heal us. Help us to forgive our family members and ignore their bad habits, as they so often forgive ours.

Prudence ~ Boot Camp Day 18: Reframing the Day

Task: Change your attitude about something you don't like.

"Offer praise as your sacrifice to God; fulfill your vows to the Most High." Psalm 50:14

I am an under-my-breath complainer. I complain about the messy house, the piles of dishes, my husband's long hours and the kids' behavior—and don't get me started about the laundry!

Laundry is my pet peeve. There is always too much. No one reuses their towels. (I have even tried hiding them and charging the kids a quarter when they need a new one, to no avail.) Almost every day I rant and rave at my kids about the amount of laundry they have "dumped" on me. Today, I tried to be different.

I washed dried and folded 6 loads of laundry in between housework, appointments and writing. Here's the kicker though, I tried to do it with a good attitude as tangible proof of my love for my family members.

It worked out all right. I hope I can remember this when I start to get bugged about little things. When I wash dishes, I can remember when I didn't have a big, beautiful family and only my dish sat in the sink. When I pick up the dog hair, reflecting on how happy my two dogs make me (and the whole family) my attitude can change. I guess I just needed a major attitude adjustment and I tried to start today.

PRAYER

Lord, You hung on a cross for us and yet, sometimes, we have trouble with doing chores for our family. Forgive us for complaining and help us to do all for You and for our family with a loving attitude.

Prudence ~ Boot Camp Day 19: Fixing Ourselves

Task: Start targeting specific individual behaviors that are getting in the way of family unity. Make a plan to start to change these behaviors.

"For just as through the disobedience of one the many were made sinners, so through the obedience of one the many will be made righteous." Romans 5:19

> You have been graced! I saw you practice the virtue of_____ when you_____.

Consider identifying the top one or two issues that your family would like to work on for each family member. If the children are old enough, ask them what things they would like to change in their own behavior. Be sure to include yourselves (parents) when you identify areas that need change. For example: dad doesn't always use appropriate language when he is angry, mom isn't a great housekeeper, oldest child doesn't remember to do their chores and youngest child screams too much.

Look at what behavior you would desire in each of these cases; identify the virtue that behavior would instill. Use this as a guide to change behavior and measure success. Dad could become more patient, mom more diligent, oldest child could also work on diligence and youngest could work on love of others.

Use the virtues and desired behaviors in an active examination of conscience each day. Utilize this when the family goes to receive the Sacrament of Reconciliation (Confession).

Consider pairing up the family members as prayer partners and using a secret 'grace' system to encourage the desired virtue. Grace cards can be made up and given anonymously to family members when they demonstrate the virtue they are working on. For example: Dad sees oldest child take out the garbage without reminder. He gives that child a 'grace card' that says, "You have been graced! I saw you work on the virtue of diligence when you took out the trash this morning!"

The last step in the plan would be to create a consequence when a bad behavior was demonstrated. Dad puts a dollar in a little bank to be donated to charity when he utters a bad word. Mom does an extra chore when she has left the dishes until morning.

PRAYER

Lord, we come to You and confess the same things time and again. Grant us the tools and grace to make permanent changes in ourselves.

Before moving on to Temperance, insights from the family boot camp activities on Prudence:

_____

_____

_____

_____

_____

_____

_____

_____

_____

_____

_____

_____

_____

_____

_____

_____

_____

_____

_____

_____

_____

_____

"Be patient with everyone, but above all with yourself. Do not lose courage in considering your own imperfections but instantly set about remedying them— every day begin the task anew."

St. Francis de Sales

Focus is on the Virtue of Temperance (Days 20 through 22)

Temperance is the virtue of moderation. When we develop this virtue we learn to control ourselves especially around sins dealing with abuse of sexual pleasure, anger and even gluttony. All families experience temptation, this virtue can help us to be strong against those issues.

Temperance ~ Boot Camp Day 20: Making a Choice to Love

Task: Choose to be kind when someone is not treating you kindly.

"A soothing tongue is a tree of life, but a perverse one crushes the spirit." Proverbs 15:4

We had another bad day recently. Anya yelled, I yelled, the other kids started feeding off the chaos and soon it seemed like the entire household was shouting.

When you raise a child with a form of autism you do not always automatically receive the love or response that you expect from her. Sometimes I am moved by love for her, I reach out to her and she (due to sensory issues) recoils. My heart falls. Other times I try so hard to understand her point of view, but it is based in a world that doesn't work like mine and frustration reigns on both sides.

Then there are the laughs and joys, too. The day she actually played with another child for the first time. I wanted to shout it to the world, but the world wouldn't understand why it was so important. She makes me laugh. My sweet little girl takes the world so literally. One day I told her to, "Hop into the car." and she did, hop, hop, like a bunny. Another time the radio announcer reminded everyone to, "Get up on the right side of the bed tomorrow." She looked puzzled and said, "If I don't get up on the right side of my bed, I'll be under my sister's bed." (They share a trundle and she sleeps on the lower part.) These things endear my little girl to me. I love her so much. I'm sorry I reacted so badly to my daughter that morning. I pray the Lord will help me to do a better job.

PRAYER

Lord, loving someone who isn't showing you love is so hard. How did You do it? We hung You on the cross and yet You loved us as You suffered. Help us to love like You do, even when we are suffering.

Temperance ~ Boot Camp Day 21: Practice Makes Perfect

Task: Practice modifying a behavior.

"Or if one loves justice, the fruits of her works are virtues;
For she teaches moderation and prudence, justice and fortitude."
Wisdom 8:7

Addictions are difficult to admit and even more difficult to overcome. Some are addicted to things like pornography, alcohol, or drugs. But all of us suffer from some form of addiction; we just call them 'bad habits.' I, myself, am addicted to a short-temper. I give in to outbursts, when I should work harder at restraining myself. One of my sons has a habit of always saying the last word. He will literally be muttering it under his breath, if he can't say it out loud (because he was just reprimanded about it). My youngest daughter screams at the drop of a hat, and so on and so on.

Any addiction or bad habit takes a lot of work to overcome. The first step is realizing that YOU are the problem. My husband likes to tell a joke about a man who was a drunk. He says, "If you had my life, you'd drink too." The irony of course, is that the man made his own situation worse by drinking! I used to say, "The kids made me so mad today." My grandpa would always remind me that no one can "make" you mad. You allow yourself to get angry and respond inappropriately. While we cannot be responsible for some of the things that happen to us, we do have the responsibility of controlling how we react to those things.

After identifying the bad behavior, the next step is to look for the things that trigger your bad habits. Once you recognize them, you have more power over them.

We practice writing and baseball, why not behavior? Our family Psychologist, Dr. Eugene McCabe, gave this wonderful idea to us. This concept is simple. Find the appropriate behavior and *practice* it at times when misbehavior is not occurring. For example: our daughter, Anya, is very loud. She does not regulate her speech well in tempo or volume. So when we are just sitting around with her we have her practice her voices. A number one voice is a whisper, two is normal, three is loud, four is louder and five is shouting. When we are *not* stressed by her shouting is the perfect time to work on this issue. Then when she gets loud we can remind her to use her #2 voice—or whatever is appropriate for the given situation. I have used this technique with simple things such as putting a cup gently in the sink by practicing picking it up and laying it down easily—or even answering the phone.

We can use this idea to role-play situations with our older children too. How do you react when someone uses God's name in vain around you? How do you answer when a friend wants you to take part in some behavior you know is wrong?

PRAYER

Lord, we are grateful for opportunities to practice good behavior with our families. Help us to remember this technique when we feel locked into bad habits. Teach us to practice virtues to overcome these habits.

*If your family had identified a serious addiction, seek help from a priest, physician or mental health professional to get the appropriate help in overcoming that problem.

Temperance ~ Boot Camp Day 22: Developing an Attitude of Chastity and Respect
Task: Discuss developing an attitude of chastity with your family.

"Immorality or any impurity or greed must not even be mentioned among you, as is fitting among holy ones," Eph. 5:3

The world tries to pull our family apart with images that are sexual and inappropriate. We can't separate ourselves completely from the world and I can't even guarantee that if we make all the right moves that our children will not give in to worldly temptations, but we can strengthen our family against these influences.

As parents, we have great influence, not only by what we say, but by our own example. My husband and I can choose to dress modestly, treat each other with respect, and not make inappropriate sexual comments to each other. We can demonstrate the values of a true Christian marriage and discuss openly with our children our decision to respect and be open to life by using natural family planning. By practicing this, we are giving our children an example of chastity. If we can respect each other enough to abstain from relations (when pregnancy is not a sought-after option at that time), then our children know they can have the strength to abstain from sexual relations when they are not married.

We believe in being open at our home and to teach with a sense of humor. In one dinner-time discussion about sex, my husband joked with the kids that they could refer to it as "monkey business" if it embarrassed them to use the actual words. Well, this turned into "funny business" and on it went until our young son, Vladimir, exclaimed, "Or you could call it···**None** of your business!" This is still a running joke in our home.

Today's teens are growing up in a world of sex-ting (sending explicit pictures or messages over cell phones), Internet porn and cavalier attitudes about sex and respect. If we don't develop the right attitude about these things at home, where will their information come from? Don't be afraid to talk about how we should dress, talk, act, and even what jokes we should and should not tell.

Several of our teens and preteens have gone through the *Theology of the Body for Teens program*. Our oldest daughter has read every book on chastity out there and is a strong pro-life advocate. We believe these things are linked because sex and babies are linked, so understanding the issues helps promote chastity. Does this mean they won't make mistakes and even possibly have sex before marriage? No. We have come to realize that we are all human and kids mess up, but we can give them a suit of spiritual and educational armor to guard themselves from the temptations of the world. This is where prayer, trust and the mercy of God come in. Do what you can, teach what you can, then entrust your children, your spouse and yourself to the fidelity of God. He will help us guard against the negative influences of the world.

Many couples hold back from using Natural Family Planning out of fear. The wife fears that her husband will not be satisfied by a decrease in the opportunity to be together. The husband fears the wife will become pregnant. It is important to discuss these issues and talk to an NFP counselor so that misconceptions (pardon the pun) do not occur. In our relationship, we discovered that we actually increased the 'special time' we were together. Because we became very protective about those 'non-fertile' times, we spent time together as often as opportunity would allow. We have even shipped the little ones off to Grandma's for just an hour, in the middle of the day, so that we could be together. (Something that we may have been reluctant to do, if we didn't view our time together as valuable, precious and limited.)

Discussing this issue and finding ways to remain chaste and pure of heart within the marital sexual relationship is a wonderful opportunity to unite your selves as a team of husband and wife.

<u>PRAYER</u>
Lord, keep all members of our family firm in their faith and in their commitment to fidelity and chastity. Remind us that our fertility is not a curse, but a gift from You to be treasured. Help us to be strong examples to our children, with the help of Your grace.

Focus is on the Virtue of Fortitude (Days 23 through 26)

Fortitude is often referred to as courage or long-suffering. I don't think that there is a family member alive that hasn't felt the need for an increase in this virtue. Some families have more challenges than others, but we can all benefit from working on the virtue of fortitude.

Fortitude ~ Boot Camp Day 23: Actions Speak Louder Than Words.
Task: Do a favor for someone in your family and tell them it is to express appreciation.

"...giving thanks always and for everything in the name of our Lord Jesus Christ to God the Father." Eph. 5:20

I call myself the invisible mom. My kids call me, "Mom, I need···" Most of the time I don't mind. My husband reminds me that when a job is done well, we rarely notice the person doing it. It is only when a job is poorly done that we look for someone to blame.

However, it can be disappointing and even hurtful when the members in our family don't appreciate what we do. When my kids say, "Thanks, Mom," it does please me, but they are still just words.

My husband gets up and works hard to provide for us every day. He likes it when I remember to thank him for his hard work, but he really appreciates it when I demonstrate my appreciation. For example, I may make a special dinner and remark that I made it specifically because he works so hard all day. My actions make my words of gratitude that much stronger.

When I see one of my children going out of the way to help another I can tell them that I am pleased with their effort, but how much more does it mean when I take the time to spend some special time with them and let them know that I am doing it to express my thanks for their consideration of their sibling.

PRAYER
Lord, help us to appreciate all that our family members do for us every day.

Fortitude ~ Boot Camp Day 24: What Does Discipline Mean?

Task: Review methods of discipline in your family and their effectiveness or ineffectiveness.

"Train a boy up in the way he should go: even when he is old, he will not swerve from it." Proverbs 22:6

Parenting is a tough job. In addition, it is the most important job we will ever perform. It is vital to do it well. Education is invaluable in raising children. A basic understanding of child development, parenting styles and discipline techniques will make the job easier. Another piece of the puzzle is knowing the goal of discipline. The root word of discipline is disciple, which means to teach. Punishment (while necessary at times) is not the goal of discipline—correction is the goal.

It is important to note that discipline issues can be approached from a team-building standpoint as well. We have recently enlisted the help of some of our older children to help the younger ones practice certain desirable behaviors (i.e. not touching other peoples things, using respectful voices to Mom and Dad etc.). This encourages the little ones and builds bonds between the children. The older children gain insight into how challenging parenting can be and they increase their tolerance for the younger ones' annoying behaviors.

No matter what methods of discipline we use and how effective we are at it, kids are going to push limits, and sometimes be downright naughty. Remember, that's *their* job! They are checking for their limits, safety nets, seeing how much we love them and trying to grow into their own person. It's a tough job for them and we have to be there to help them find their way. I have found it helpful to say to myself, "That's the stage he/she is in. It's normal for that age group." Acknowledging that their behavior is not necessarily personal helps me to cope and become proactive and supportive, rather than reactive and negative.

When they seem to hate us most, they need us the most. Recently, after fighting with me, my adult daughter came up to me and said, "Thanks for all you do and the mom you are, now I need a mommy hug." Those are the moments we hang onto. Then you know it is all worthwhile.

PRAYER
Dearest Father, You are a father too! You have to discipline us all the time. When we disobey, we stand in the way of Your grace. It seems like we confess the same sins time and time again. Help us to remember this struggle when disciplining our own children. Give us

the grace to discipline in love, not anger. Help us to keep in mind the goal of disciplining is to correct and teach, not to punish. Thank You for these children and trusting us to raise them.

Goals of Discipline

A basic understanding of how children develop can help parents decide what discipline techniques will work for them. When examining Piaget's Preoperational Stages of Development, Erickson's Stage Theory and Freud's idea of the Id, Ego and Superego some common ideas emerge. The following is an overview of these different theories of child development.

Birth-1year: *Goal of discipline: Redirecting child.*

Child is learning about self and environment. Child is centered on self. Parents and siblings are child's favorite toy. Child thinks concretely. Child starts testing if outcomes are reliable (drops spoon, mom picks up, drops spoon again). Separation anxiety visible at around 6-8 months.

2-3 years old: *Goal of discipline: Redirecting child; starting to teach using small phrases.*

Child is attempting self-sufficiency, discovering own power, developing language, using symbols to represent objects and ideas. Child is still very focused on self, but starting to see interaction with world and forming limited abstract thoughts. Exploring and testing are common behaviors at this age.

4-6 years old: *Goal of discipline: Teaching, helping child internalize rules and expectations.*

Child is gaining empathy for others, understanding many abstract concepts, looking at self and beginning to look at moral self (good vs. bad, right vs. wrong).

6-puberty: *Goal of discipline: Increase child's understanding of rules and reasons for them, decrease undesirable behavior and begin self-monitoring.*

Child is learning to function socially, continuing to explore abstract ideas, increasing empathy for others, learning to look at other points of view. Developing sense of self.

Adolescence: *Goal of discipline: Self monitoring and child is able to make positive choices.*

Child is separating from parents, exploring own identity, learning to manage life on their own.

It is very important to note here that children who have certain conditions and/or disabilities may not fall into the 'norms' of child development. For those children we need to apply a different standard and adjust our expectations appropriately.

Fortitude ~ Boot Camp Day 25: I Can't Hear You When You Yell
Task: Make a choice not to yell today.

"For a father's blessing, gives a family firm roots, but a mother's curse uproots the growing plant." Sirach 3:9

I start each day with a prayer for patience. I vow not to yell or overreact. Why is it then that I can barely make it through a single day without "losing it" at one point or another?

Many parents identify with Martha's struggle (Luke 10:38) between the work of running a home and the desire to sit quietly listening to our Lord. We long to sit and hold our children, seeing the Lord in their faces, hearing His voice in theirs. There are so many needs that it is easy to become overwhelmed. My husband calls it, "a convergence of simultaneous demands." When I am unable to find peace of mind amidst the confusion, I find myself on the verge of becoming the wife and mother I do not want to be.

I cry by their beds at night for my sins of impatience and a quick temper, praying silently for the grace to do better tomorrow as I kiss their sweet smelling, damp foreheads. I question God's plan in giving me these children. Surely, someone else would do a better job. Somewhere in the darkness and in my heart I hear His answer. He gave them to me because it is part of His perfect will.

In a survey of parents in the March 1995 issue of *Child Magazine*, 37% admitted to yelling at their children to discipline them, while only 1% rated it as effective.

In a more recent study quoted in *Better Homes and Garden's* August 2004 issue, Murray A. Straus, professor of sociology at University of New Hampshire found that 74% of parents surveyed reported yelling or screaming at their kids (the 2003 study was published in the *Journal of Marriage and Family*).

In *The Catholic Family Handbook*, by Reverend Lawrence G. Lovasik (Sophia Institute Press, 1962-updated 2000) it states, "Anger at misbehavior never works because you are not helping your child to face and get out his anger."

Scripture reminds us, "I tell you, on the day of judgment people will render an account for every careless word they speak. By your words you will be acquitted, by your words you will be condemned." Matt 12:36-37

This is a difficult habit to defeat. Going to the sacrament of Reconciliation regularly provides the necessary grace we need to overcome it. My son's teacher is very good at lowering her voice when the class gets louder. Practicing this at home may help to decrease the amount of yelling. Just taking a breath, counting to ten and having a cup of tea may help increase our ability to deal with the stress that usually leads to raised voices.

Prayer

Lord, help each of us to identify the causes of our anger today. Please help us to hold our tongues and not to utter a careless word to those around us. Help us to seek solutions, not become part of the problem. Help our family to speak kindly to one another and to be patient with each other's faults. Lord, I know that each of us is your child, help all of us to feel your constant love today. Thank you for loving us.

Fortitude ~ Boot Camp Day 26: Learning to Communicate

Task: Introduce a new way of communicating to your family.

"Therefore, putting away falsehood, speak the truth, each one to his neighbor, for we are members one of another." Eph. 4:25

"Come here right now!" I shouted to my-then three-year-old daughter. "I'm not playing games with you anymore!" She immediately burst into tears, "You aren't going to play dolly or tea party ever again?" My little girl had taken me literally and I had hurt her with my words.

Poor communication is most often stated as a reason for family conflict and ultimately the failure of many marriages. Many people have not been taught proper techniques to improve communication in their own lives. As with my example, meanings can be misunderstood and feelings can be hurt. I have often witnessed 'text fights' among my children and their friends. In these days of instant messaging, email and texting, opportunities for miscommunication are even greater.

One technique we have learned is to say *why* you are about to say something before you say it. For instance, if I just need to vent to my husband (and not for him to 'fix' anything), I can say, "Hey, Sweetie, I need to share some things with you that are going on with me. I don't need you to do anything, I just really want to talk and share with you what I'm going through." My young adult daughter, Katya, is very good at doing this. She'll say, "I don't really need your opinion on this, I just want to share." Other times, some action may be needed and that is equally important. Just clarifying what the expectations of the conversation are can help.

Developing fair rules for fighting can help too. Let's face it, disagreements will happen; but, there can still be rules about how to handle these arguments. We agree not to call each other names, not to bring up past issues, and not to bring the dog's name into any of our fights. (Okay, the last one is a family joke, but it actually is on paper and hangs on our fridge).

PRAYER

Lord, teach us to control what we say to each other and how we communicate. Help us to strengthen each other with our words.

Communication Techniques

The Talking Stick: A communication technique that can help couples and families talk to each other is the (Native American) talking stick idea. Use a stick, spoon or whatever else works for you. The object is given to the speaker. No one else can speak until the person holding the object has fully expressed him or herself.

Written Dialogue: This is a format that is used frequently in Marriage Encounter weekends. A subject or question is given. Each spouse writes his/her response or thoughts about the subject (for about 10-20 minutes) and then the spouses exchange letters, read and discuss them. The benefit of this format is that each person can process and express their thoughts completely and without immediate fear of repercussion. Then each can quietly process what the other has written. It is a thoughtful, less reactive approach to communication.

The Mirror: One more helpful way to increase communication between family members is the 'mirror' approach. One person expresses him or herself and another states what that person has just said. For example: "I wish you wouldn't leave your clothes on the bathroom floor all the time. It is a mess!" The (offending) spouse answers, "I hear that you do not appreciate the way I leave my clothes on the bathroom floor. I will try to be more considerate of your feelings and the work you have done to keep the bathroom clean, and remember to pick up my clothes."

Humor: Humor is a wonderful way to break the tension when communicating. It must be administered gently, without any sarcasm (especially when talking to your spouses or teenage children), but it can change the direction a conversation is going in a heartbeat. I remember one instance when we were very upset with our teenage son for some bad grades. He yelled at us, "Fine, I'll just be a bum!" I realized the argument was escalating, so I put my hand on his shoulder and told him, "I believe in you and I know that if you really try, you can be the best bum there ever was." He immediately laughed and we all calmed down.

Focus is on the Virtue of Faith (Days 27 through 30)

The virtue of Faith helps us to believe in God and all that He has revealed to us including what the Catholic Church teaches. Families need more than one kind of faith, faith in God and faith in each other. This last section will concentrate on ways to increase our faith within our families.

Faith ~ Boot Camp Day 27: Pray First
Task: Make prayer a priority.

"Pray without ceasing." 1 Thes. 5:17

"Pray hard! Katya's hurt and she's not moving." The words of my-then 12 year-old-son echoed in my head. I ran out to the backyard to see my 5 year-old daughter lying unconscious in my husband's arms. Somewhere in my mind it registered that I had screamed her name and that could be the only prayer I would have time to offer up to God.

In that moment, my son taught us a valuable lesson, *always pray first.* My husband was able to resuscitate our daughter and she suffered no permanent damage from her injury. After the incident I marveled at how all our children automatically began to pray for their sister when they saw her get hurt.

Do I always call out "Abba, Father, help me," before I try anything else, or is it often my last step? I forget or wait until I have exhausted my own resources, then, in desperation, I cry out to God. My children acted upon faith and instinct—often the way little children pray.

Of course, not every situation is a crisis moment; even in the routine of everyday life we can find time to pray...

When our kids were little we had trouble getting them all to fall asleep, so we started a tradition that lasted for years. We would tuck them into their beds, and then my husband and I would sit

"Pray as if all depends on God, work as if all depends on you."
St. Ignatius Loyola

in the hallway and (loudly) say the Rosary. Bedtime problems disappeared; my children all learned the Rosary and enjoyed the night time routine. Today, we use time in the car on trips or on our way to Mass to say the Rosary together.

Another prayer tradition in our family is our blessing. Whenever we say goodbye or goodnight, we make the sign of the cross on each other's foreheads and pray, "May God bless you and keep you and bring you safely home at the end of the day." When my father-in-law lay dying, these words and this blessing took on a new and more important meaning Rocking a sick child and meditating on Mary rocking baby Jesus in her arms can also become a prayer. There is time and opportunity for prayer in everyday moments; we only have to look for them.

PRAYER
Lord, help us to make time for prayer and to recognize hidden opportunities to pray.

Ways to Pray as a Family

➤ Lunch with the Lord
  o Place a Bible verse with a short meditation in a child's or spouse's lunchbox.
➤ Make receiving the Sacraments a family affair
  o Consider putting aside one Saturday a month to go to Confession as a family. By participating with our children, we set a good example and the whole family is blessed with actual and sanctifying grace.
➤ Offer it up
  o Learning to offer up pain, suffering and frustrations can help us to grow in prayer and faith. My children have heard me scream, "Lord, help me in this moment RIGHT NOW!" They have learned that God is big enough to handle our good times and our bad.

Faith ~ Boot Camp Day 28: Mass Appeal
Task: Go to Mass as a Family.

"For My flesh is true food and My blood is true drink. Whoever eats My flesh and drinks My blood remains in Me and I in him."
John 6:55,56

One of my favorite lines in a movie is when the hero declares his love by saying, "You complete me." I thought about this the other day during the Consecration of the Eucharist.

I was feeling very damaged that day at Mass. Not whole at all. I wanted to cry and I really didn't even feel like being there. Then, it happened: Transubstantiation. Jesus was there, present in the Eucharist!! Nothing seemed to matter at that moment. I didn't need to be perfect, or even happy, I just needed to be *there*.

As I received Communion I felt myself thinking, "You complete me." He can be with me and fill up everything that is lacking. Jesus alone can give me the grace to take the next step, even when my weary soul doesn't really want to or seem to have the wherewithal needed for the task. He can accomplish works through me that I didn't think were possible. What a gift we Catholics have in the Eucharist!

To instill this love of the Eucharist in our families, we have to remind them frequently that Jesus *really is there*. It is so easy for us to get complacent and forget that He is present, Body, Blood, Soul and Divinity. If you are like me, your mind wanders to what I am making for dinner or why my kids are being so squirmy. I am so easily distracted during Mass, but when I remind myself that my King is present it is easier to refocus.

Teaching our families stories about Eucharistic miracles and Saints who love Jesus in the Eucharist may make the experience more real for them too. Many (Church approved) Eucharistic Miracles have been documented. In Italy, the Eucharist turned into visible flesh and blood during the Consecration.

"This miracle has undergone extensive scientific examination and can only be explained as a miracle. The flesh is actually cardiac tissue which contains arterioles, veins, and nerve fibers. The blood type as in all other approved Eucharistic miracles is type AB!" (http://www.therealpresence.org/eucharst/mir/a3.html)

Or consider St. Tarcisius, he was a 12 year-old boy who lived during the third century in Rome. He was given the task of secretly bringing Communion to Christian prisoners sentenced to die. Tarcisius was attacked by a group of boys and he was killed trying to protect the Holy Eucharist he was carrying.

As our children get older we may hear, "Mass is boring, what's the point? Why are you making me go?" I had this conversation with my own son just the other day.

I explained to him that I wasn't trying to force something on him; rather I wanted to share something I love with him. You see, I absolutely love chocolate cream pie! If it was up to me, we would have it for dessert every Sunday night. When you really like something, it makes you happy and satisfied. When that happens you want to share that experience with everyone. I even can't imagine someone that has never tried chocolate cream pie not wanting to give it a try. I think that once someone really tastes it, they'll love it. In fact, I can imagine myself getting a little insistent when trying to get someone to try it. "Oh, it is SO good, just try it! Maybe just a little bite. Please, for me!"

I love Mass. I love knowing the Lord is there. He talks to me in His Word and then feeds me in His Eucharist. I feel happy and satisfied. I want to share it with everyone I know. What may look like nagging may actually be just wanting to share something that is so very good.

I have also observed (especially in myself) that we focus a lot on what we need God's help with and yet we rarely ask God what He needs help with. Does He need us to be more observant of someone else's needs? Is He asking us to feed the hungry? Does He want us to take a risk and change something? How can Mass be a two-way relationship if we are only coming there to get something and not to give or offer help? If we are active participants we may not find Mass tedious at all. When we are listening (and not just asking) we may hear God's voice in our hearts.

Mass, unlike chocolate cream pie, is a relationship. It is a beautiful dance between us and the Lord. He leads, we follow. He comes with love and gifts to woo us and we respond with a desire to please Him.

Mass is as beautiful as love and as pleasing as chocolate cream pie. These two things make it irresistible to me.

PRAYER
Lord, set our hearts on fire for You, especially in the Eucharist! Bring our family closer together as we attend Mass together. Help us to attend Mass, not only on Sundays and Holy Days of Obligation, but on weekdays when ever we can.

Faith ~ Boot Camp Day 29: The Word of God
Task: Study Scripture as a family.

"You are my refuge and shield; in your word I hope." Psalm 119:114

Along with enjoying the privilege of receiving Christ in the Eucharist, Catholics should be aware of the beauty in studying the Bible. While it is true that many Catholics do not actively study the Bible on their own, many others do. There are great tools for this in Catholic books stores and online. If you are a Catholic currently not studying His Word, this is the time to research sources that will allow you to do this with reverence and spark a love affair with Scripture! If nothing else, begin by visiting a website such as http://usccb.org/ which makes the daily readings available right at your fingertips!

Our family believes that in order to better serve Christ; we must know God in His Word. We often challenge our children to find a Bible story that represents a situation we are going through and when they were little, we used to have them memorize Bible verses. This is always an area we can do more in, BUT Catholics do know their Bibles because of the Mass.

During the Mass the Bible is covered in a three year cycle. This includes the Gospels, much of the Old Testament and the New Testament. While not everything is completely read, the focus on the Word of God cannot be denied. Besides that fact, much of the prayers during the Mass and the responses are directly from the Bible.

Catholics are also privileged to have the fullness of the faith. The Mass is separated into two parts: The Liturgy of the Word and The Liturgy of the Eucharist. We tell our children to think of it this way; if you wanted to get to know our family, we might share with you a book of love letters we have written to each other. Or perhaps, those of you reading this are starting to feel like you know us already! How much better will we know each other, if after reading, we all have dinner together? You will hear the tone of our voices as we laugh and share. You will see our craziness (and at our house even some bad behavior).

How much better can we know the Lord then if we read His Word and then come to His table and share in His supper?! A great way to start is to read *Ephesians.* In this book in the New Testament, we are given an outline on how to live as Christians in family life.

PRAYER
Lord, inspire us to get to know You better through Your Word. Help us to make time for You.

Faith ~ Boot Camp Day 30: Remembering Our Commitment to Christ

Task: Have a recommitment ceremony, consecrating your family to the Sacred Heart of Jesus, through the Immaculate Heart of Mary.

*"Commit your way to the Lord;
trust that God will act and make your integrity shine like the dawn,
your vindication like noonday."
Psalm 37:5,6*

"A glimpse of heaven." That is how my husband described the day we decided to have a recommitment ceremony.

Where do I start in explaining the miracles that day brought? Let me start with our oldest daughter. She had attended a Catholic retreat; she had been in pain, and searching desperately for something to hold on to. You see, Valentine's Day marked the anniversary of her brain surgery. It is always a tough time for her, but for some reason, this year she was really struggling.

As she prepared for the retreat, she got into a minor car accident. She said that 'evil' was trying to prevent her from going. On that retreat, she found a renewed faith and a very special person. The day we had our ceremony, they realized that they were falling in love. It was as if our house had new life. Their joy just spread onto all of us like the wind of the Holy Spirit. We actually felt privileged to witness it.

Then, the miracles continued. We had friends over for dinner and felt blessed by their presence. They had three children (under the age of three years-old) and my kids just took over. They watched them, played with them, and loved them. I saw my children shine and it made my heart swell with happiness. Our friends melted into the peacefulness of letting others love and care for their babies.

Still, more: A young man (who became our unofficial foster son) was having serious issues at his home. He was leaving for the military soon, right after high school graduation, but for that time, he was a little displaced. My husband opened our home to him and invited him to stay with us whenever he needs to. He looked as if he had been wrapped up in a warm blanket. He smiled and played with the younger kids. He knew he was loved.

Our house brimmed with love and our cup runneth over. We decided to use that moment to recommit ourselves to Christ. We lit a candle. We included all those in our home and they took part in our ceremony. We again promised to love and serve the Lord. We asked the Lord to make up in us the things that keep us from loving each other more fully and we pledged to continue His work here on earth.

FINAL PRAYER

Lord, is saying "Thank You" enough? How can we ever thank you for the gift of your love, sacrifice and our salvation through You? Thank You. We love You. Help us to show that in the way we treat each other. Thank You for this time in which our hope was in You, our faith was in You and our trust was in You. May we all continue to live our lives as Your Sons and Daughters, fully aware of Your presence in every person, in every situation; and may the fruits of this time continue to grow throughout our lives. In Jesus' name, we thank You.

Final thoughts...

_____

_____

_____

_____

_____

_____

_____

_____

_____

_____

_____

_____

_____

_____

_____

_____

_____

_____

_____

Bibliography

Bellet, Marie, *Thy Will be Done*, What I Wanted to Say, Elm St. Records, 1997

Benkovic, Johnnette, Living His Life Abundantly Newsletter, April 2004

Catechism of the Catholic Church, 1994 Libria Editrice Vaticana Citta del Vaticano

Gardner, Mary Ann, *A Parent's Way of the Cross*, Marian Mantle, October 2003

Kendrick, Stephen and Kendrick, Alex, The Love Dare, Nashville, TN: B and H Publishing Group, 2008

Lovasik, Lawrence G., The Catholic Family Handbook, Sophia Institute Press,1962(2000)

New American Bible, St. Joseph Edition, New York: Catholic Book Publishing Co.,1970 edition

Pope John Paul II, Letter to Families, February 1974

Pope John Paul II, Apostolic Letter, Mulieris Dignitatem, August 1988

Pope Paul VI, Humanae Vitae, July 25, 1968

Second Vatican Council, pastoral conts. Guadium et Spes, No. 50

Websites

Family Life Center International and St. Joseph Covenant Keepers, www.dads.org.

Al-Anon, www.alanon.org

CPSIA information can be obtained at www.ICGtesting.com
Printed in the USA
LVOW090748160513

333935LV00001B/6/P